C0-AJR-516

Merak T. Kasuya

Headmaster of Ichiyo School

Tokyo

Imaginative Ikebana

by Meikof Kasuya

Founder and Headmaster, Ichjyo School of Floral Art
Director of Japan Federation of Ikebana Artists
Honorary Member of Royal Horticultural Society

JAPAN PUBLICATIONS, INC.

© 1970 by Meikof Kasuya. All rights reserved.
Published by Japan Publications, Inc.
JAPAN PUBLICATIONS TRADING CO., 1255 Howard St., San Francisco, Calif. 94103 U.S.A.
P. O. Box 5030 Tokyo International, Tokyo, Japan. Library of Congress Catalog Card No.
72-136640
First Printing: November 1970

Photographs by Mitsuyoshi Kasuya
Printed in Japan by Toppan Printing Co., Ltd

Contents

Foreword   3

CREATIVE ARRANGEMENTS BY THE AUTHOR   4
BASIC IKEBANA ART PRINCIPLES   6
THE THREE-VIEW ARRANGEMENT IN THE ICHIYO SCHOOL
    METHOD—Applied Style I   8
  Placement of Ikebana Arrangements   10
  Step-by-step Explanation   11
  Variations of the Three-view Form   12
THE FLOWING FORM—Applied Style II   14
  Step-by-step Explanation   15
  More Variations on the Flowing Form   17
  The Beauty of the Curve in Ikebana   18
  Further Variations on the Flowing Form
    Additional *Kenzan*   20
  Flowing Form Using Dried Materials   21
  Flowing Form Variations Using Tall Containers   22
  Another Application of the Flowing Form—Double Containers   24
COMBINATION FORM (Two Containers)—Applied Style III   26
  Variations on Hanging Combination Form A   28
  Variations on Slanting Combination Form B   29
  Variations on the Combination Form in Two-Mouth
    Containers   32
  Step-by-step Explanation   31
  Further Variations on Combination Form in Two-mouth
    Containers   33
HEAVEN-EARTH FORM—Applied Style IV   34
  Variations on Heaven-earth Form A   36
  Step-by-step Explanation   38
  Variations on the Heaven-earth Form   39, 41
  More Variations on the Heaven-earth Form   40
CROSSING FORM—Applied Style V   42
  Example of the Crossing Form   43
  Illustrations of the Crossing Form   44
  Variations on the Crossing Form   48
  Step-by-step Explanation   47
  Variations on the Crossing Form—Tall Narrow Style   48
  Step-by-step Explanation   50
GROUP-CONTRAST FORM—Applied Style VI   52
  Variations on Group-contrast Form   53
  Step-by-step Explanation   54
  Variations on the Group-contrast Form   56
PREPARING LEAVES AND FLOWERS FOR ARRANGEMENT   58
  Tips For Keeping Arrangements Fresh   61
  Preserving Leaves   61

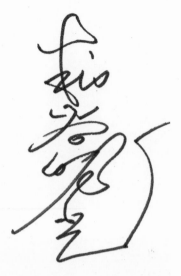

Foreword

There are various methods of studying the art of ikebana, but in the Ichiyo School there are three distinct stages of study: beginning, intermediate, and advanced. These stages have definite basic rules, and it is essential that they be carefully learned and practiced if one wishes to make the study of ikebana an exploration of art in its highest form. The Ichiyo method requires that the foundations of these three stages be carefully layed.

My earlier book, *Introducing Ikebana*, explained the fundamental steps of beginning ikebana; the present intermediate volume emphasizes six different applied forms. In each of them, the true meaning of ikebana is manifested. Within these six forms, hundreds of arrangements can be created, and through their application the true art of ikebana in all of its creativeness will emerge.

The basic rules and Ichiyo method of arrangement of each form are thoroughly explained. Beginning with the first step, the progression is clearly set forth. Illustrations show the exact method of structuring each applied form. The basic rules are not for the purpose of restricting the choice of materials, containers, placement, general effect, inspiration, or creativeness; instead they give the arranger a new freedom of self-expression. As in all arts, in ikebana too the essential basic rules and concepts must be mastered before the personalized beauty of the creation becomes a new, different, and imaginative arrangement.

Tokyo,
August, 1970

Creative Arrangements by the Author

In ikebana, the expression of contrast creates some of the most beautiful and interesting arrangements. In this two-mouth container, an original design by the author and one that is used extensively by the Ichiyo School, different kinds of branches are used on the left and right to create contrast. The container is a forward slanting U shape, with one mouth slightly higher than the other. The space that results between the lines of the opposite branches is an essential part of the total effect. The chrysanthemums are added as accessories. This is an application of the Combination Form, Applied Style 3. See page 26.

Pine, Quince, and Chrysanthemums in a U-shaped Container.

In contrast to the design on the left, which was created with very few materials, this arrangement uses greater variety. With the exact placement of each branch and flower, there is, in the completed arrangement, a feeling of delicacy and finesse. It is as if one were either hearing a Bach composition or viewing a precise ballet performed with exactness and grace. This is an application of the Crossing Form, Applied Style 5. See page 42.

Hydrangea Leaves, Sansho (a Native Japanese Mountain Shrub) and Roses in a Bronze Compote Designed by the Author.

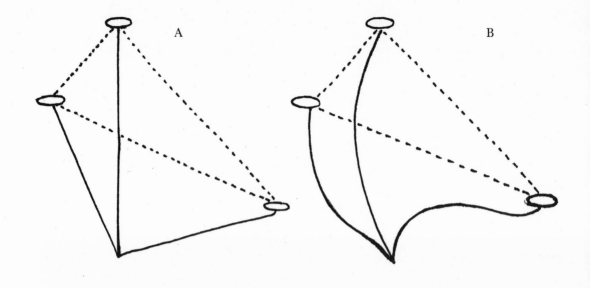

A   B

Basic Ikebana Art Principles

In all true art forms, the basic rules and principles for the creation of beauty are similar. In the Ichiyo School of Ikebana, there are three major principles that must be studied and applied:

 Beauty Created by the Use of Line
 Beauty Created by the Use of Color
 Beauty Created by the Use of Space

I. Creating Beauty of Line

In making a flower arrangement, the most essential point is the formation of line. The outline is made by the shape and direction of the main branches as they rise from the container. Line beauty can also mean surface texture or mass formation. In establishing line in ikebana, the unique Japanese concept of line balance is expressed. This is a different concept of line and balance from that usual in Western art. Whereas Western art tends to express balance by means of symmetrical equality, as in the equilateral triangle, Japanese art uses the concept of the obtuse triangle. Whether it is in the arranging of stones in a Japanese garden or the weaving of a design for a kimono, the balance is asymmetrical. This use of the idea of the obtuse triangle gives infinite variety of balance, movement, and application and, in ikebana, becomes the fascinating beauty of unbalanced balance.

BEAUTY OF LINE

Natural branches used to make the outline may or may not be the exact shape the arranger wants. Sometimes, in order to produce the desired line, the branches must be bent and shaped in different ways. The basic purpose of this book is to assist the student in understanding the techniques of bending and shaping branches to create line. This is the essential point throughout the explanation of each applied form and style.

II.   Beauty of Color

Again, as in all art, so in ikebana, the various colors of the materials used must harmonize with the basic lines. Correct combination of colors in the materials gives a pleasing effect to the completed arrangement. Color harmony and color usage vary in Japanese and Western conceptions. In the Orient, certain color combinations suggest elegance, joy, sorrow, or felicitations. Perhaps most significant, the expression of the seasons through choice of color and materials is basic in ikebana.

In decorating a home, the colors as well as the styles of the draperies, carpets, and furniture are made to harmonize. In Western dress, the color of a necktie or blouse not only harmonizes with the other apparel, but also becomes an expression of the personality of the wearer. Similarly, colors in ikebana must both harmonize with all of the other materials and express the creative idea of the arranger.

III.   Beauty of Space

Space, in ikebana, is created by the lines of the Main Stems. The Basic Flowers are designed to emphasize the beauty of the space formed.

In the beginning of the study of ikebana (see *Introducing Ikebana* by Meikof Kasuya) the placements of Basic Flowers are restricted: they are usually set at the base of an arrangement. However, in more sophisticated ikebana expression, their placement is much freer. Basic Flowers may now have a wider differentiation in height, and no rigid rules regulate their lengths. In some arrangements, Basic Flowers are used in mass effect for color emphasis. Sometimes Main Stems may be reversed and placed in the front and the Basic Flowers in the rear. The Basic Flowers can act as Assistant Stems to the Main Branches. In other words, to be truly creative in ikebana, one must be able to use the Basic Flowers in innumerable imaginative ways to develop pleasing designs. There is no limit to the use of Basic Flowers. The elementary geometrical forms are the square, the rectangle, the circle and the triangle. The simplest is the triangle, which is the basic outline of ikebana. The lines connecting the points of a triangle may be straight, or they may curve. In example A shown in page 6, the points of the obtuse triangle are joined by straight lines, whereas in example B, the same three points have been connected by curved ones.

Ikebana outline branches may be placed as in example B, but to develop more beautiful and imaginative lines, they are often bent and shaped into flowing curves, which make creative art of arrangements.

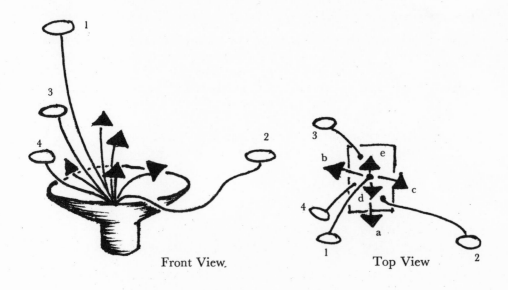

Front View.   Top View

The Three-view Arrangement in the Ichiyo School Method

APPLIED STYLE 1

FIRST MAIN STEM: Place this stem in the center of the *kenzan* between the front and side of the container. It should slant about twenty degrees towards the front.

SECOND MAIN STEM: This stem is put in the front right corner of the *kenzan* between the front and side of the container. It should slant about sixty degrees to the right.

THIRD MAIN STEM: Place this stem on the left back of the *kenzan* so that it slants about thirty degrees to the rear. It must incline in the opposite direction from that of the Second Main Stem.

FOURTH MAIN STEM: This should be put on the left front corner of the *kenzan* between the front and side of the container. Placed under the First Main Stems, it completes the triangle.

The First, Second, and Third Main Stems, if placed correctly, will form a diagonal straight line at their bases on the *kenzan*. Another diagonal straight line must be formed across the tops of the First, Second, and Third Main Stems.

In this form, either straight or curved materials may be used. They may be leaves, branches, or flowers. In addition, any kind of container—round, square, rectangular, or tall—is effective.

A broad spacious feeling results from using Four Main Stems. Since the main characteristic of this form is width it may be used wherever a wide arrangement is desired.

Main Stems: Large white chrysanthemums
Assistant Stems: White baby chrysanthemums
Basic Flowers: Yellow chrysanthemums
Container: Chinese red pottery bowl

Main Stems: Yellow chrysanthemums
Assistant Stems: None used
Basic Flowers: Red and yellow baby chrysanthemums
Container: Traditional Japanese dish

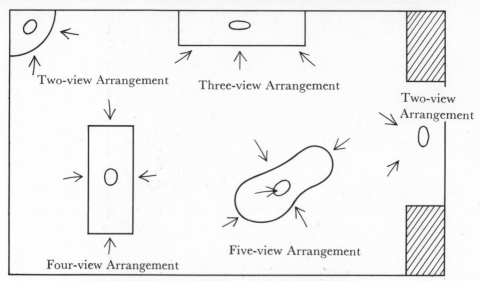

Placement of Ikebana Arrangements

TWO-VIEW ARRANGEMENT: Three Main Stems make up the outline. This kind of arrangement is best used in a shadow box or in the corner of a room, where it will be viewed from two different angles.

THREE-VIEW ARRANGEMENT: Four Main Stems make the outline for an arrangement to be seen from the front and from the left and right. It is effective on a buffet, desk, or low chest.

FOUR-VIEW ARRANGEMENT: Using Five Main Stems, this is the ideal form for a dining table or other location where it is viewed from all sides.

FIVE-VIEW ARRANGEMENT: This cluster, mass, or short-stem arrangement for shallow containers is used on coffee table, low side table, or below a stairway where it will be seen from above as well as from all sides.

Large White Chrysanthemums, White Baby Chrysanthemums and Yellow Chrysanthemums in a Chinese Red Pottery Bowl.

STEP-BY-STEP EXPLANATION

A

STEP 1.   The First Main Stem, a white chrysanthemum placed in the center of the *kenzan*, slants about twenty degrees to the left.

STEP 2.   The Second Main Stem, another white chrysanthemum, slants about sixty degrees to the right.

STEP 3.   The Third Main Stem, a third white chrysanthemum, is placed on the back left of the *kenzan*, slanting about thirty degrees opposite the Second Main Stem and forming a fan shape. This stem is a little shorter than the second one. Notice that these three stems form a diagonal straight line both on the *kenzan* and at the level of the tops of the flowers.

B

STEP 4.   The Fourth Main Stem, another white chrysanthemum, slants about forty-five degrees toward the left front. The diagonal line of the first three main stems and the added chrysanthemum form a long, wide triangle.

C

STEP 5.   Basic Flowers have been added. Their placement is most important. As shown in diagram A, the yellow chrysanthemum, put to the front of the *kenzan*, covers the *kenzan* and is the focal point of the arrangement. In Diagram B, baby chrysanthemums are inserted on the left side to point outward and to fill the open space created by the Main Stems.

Variations of the Three-view Form

The Main Stems are four aspidistra leaves; another leaf of the same plant is an Assistant Stem to the First Main Stem. The Basic Flowers are yellow chrysanthemums. See the diagram on the preceding page for the placement of the Basic Flowers.

Aspidistra Leaves and Yellow Chrysanthemums in a Triangular Pottery Vase.

Plum Blossoms, Cedar Branches (Dyed Red), and Yellow Tulips (Petals Open) in a Tall Ebony Ceramic Vase.

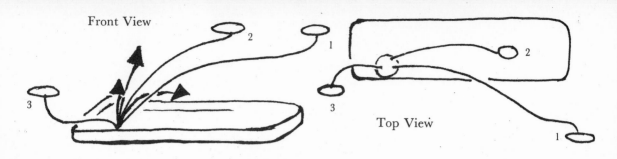

Front View

2

1

3

2

Top View

3

1

The Flowing Form

APPLIED STYLE 2

FIRST MAIN STEM: Place on the *kenzan* slanting about seventy degrees to the right and slightly forward. This low stem seems to flow across the container.

SECOND MAIN STEM: Place it to slant about forty-five degrees and to stand tall over the First Main Stem. It must flow in the same direction.

THIRD MAIN STEM: Place at about seventy degrees opposite the First Main Stem. It slants between the front and side in a flowing line away from the container.

Materials: Branches, leaves, or flowers with natural outward curves.

Container: A long, narrow oval or rectangular container.

Placement: Any long narrow area: entrance table, low chest, long coffee table, buffet, or area below a picture window.

Shortleaf Pine and Red Tulips in a Long Oval Light Blue Ceramic Container.

STEP-BY-STEP EXPLANATION

A

STEP 1.   The First Main Stem is a pine branch. Choose one with a beautiful natural curve, like the branch in the illustration. It must slant quite low at more than eighty degrees and seem to flow over water. Its direction is slightly forward.

STEP 2.   The Second Main Stem, also a pine branch, is more slender, and shorter than the First. It is placed on the back of the *kenzan* slanting fifty degrees in the same direction as the First Main Stem. It must lean directly over the container to give the same sense of flowing motion as the First Main Stem. At this juncture, it is important to adjust the placement of the *kenzan* to about either point 1 or point 9 in the container. It may be moved in any direction necessary to give proper balance; however, there must be complete harmony between the branches and the container to give the natural flowing feeling. Study the balance in the picture carefully to understand this point.

B

STEP 3.   The Third Main Stem, another pine branch placed opposite the First Main Stem, slants about eighty degrees slightly forward between the front and side of the container. A deep, strong slant is needed to create proper balance between the First and Third Main Stems.

STEP 4.   Into the wide space opened between the First and Second Main Stems, Assistant Stems, pine branches, are added.

C

STEP 5.   Add the Basic Flowers, red tulips. The color of these flowers contrasts splendidly with the dark green of the pine. This is a good technique for adding interest and enhancing color. The petals of two of the tulips have been carefully opened: all petals of the short front tulip and three of the one in the back. The third and tallest tulip remains in its natural form and, following the curved line of the Second Main Stem, slants slightly forward. See page 16 for the color illustration of this arrangement.

Shortleaf Pine and Red Tulips in a Long Oval Light Blue Ceramic Container.

The fresh roses are put in a cup of water that is placed behind the pine cone.

Green Ferns (Sprayed Gold) Pine Cones (Sprayed Silver and Gold), and Red Roses in a Narrow Silver Tray.

Young Hydrangea Branches and Orange Tiger Lilies in a Basket Made from One Piece of Split Bamboo.

The Beauty of the Curve in Ikebana
Creating Two Forms

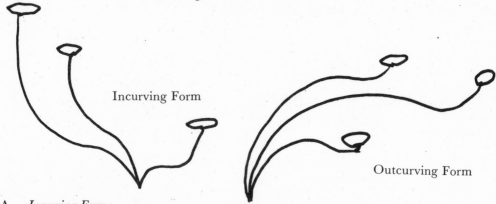

Incurving Form

Outcurving Form

A. *Incurving Form:*

Materials used in the Incurving Form harmonize with low square or round containers.

B. *Outcurving Form:*

The Outcurving Form best suits long, narrow containers.

Materials may be roughly divided into two classes: those which naturally curve inward and those which naturally curve outward. The front, or top, of the leaves of all plants seeks the energy of the sun, whereas their undersides seek moisture. The front of the leaf, then, is smooth, but the underpart is rough. In ikebana, the back of the leaf is considered unsightly. Therefore, one must study the branch to determine the directions of growth of the leaves. When branches are used as they grow, curving inward or outward, the fronts must be determined by the growth of the top of the leaves. Materials with inward curves seem to communicate strength; the outward curve has a gentler, softer feeling.

The curves of almost all branches can be changed. In fact, they can be completely reversed by using various ikebana bending techniques. Material with an incurve can be be forced to curve outward by bending and twisting the middle of the branch. Such reversals reveal the imagination and creativeness of the arranger and produce new lines. This is one of the basic conceptions that make ikebana a creative art.

Naturally Incurving Materials:

Magnolia, azalea, plum, quince, camellia, loquat, apple, cherry, dried or artificial materials.

Naturally Outcurving Materials:

Forsythia, willow, climbing rose, wisteria vine, eucalyptus, palm leaf, aspidistra leaf, hydrangea, pomegranate, rubber plant, persimmon, fern, dried or artificial materials.

Bending Technique:

Hold the branch firmly, with both hands slightly touching and with knuckles up. The branch is then twisted and bent simultaneously, until the desired curve is produced. The hands must touch, and the branch must be twisted while being bent to prevent breaking. The hands must move gradually from the base of the branch toward the tip. Repeat the process until the desired curve is obtained.

Bending Technique

Incurving material.

Bending technique.

Desired curve created.

Further Variation on the Flowing Form:
Additional *Kenzan*

Two *kenzans* are used to create a double arrangement.

Baby's Breath and Red Azalea in a Long White Glazed Vase.

To suit this arrangement to a very large area use three *kenzans*.
Materials: Phoenix—the natural shape has been modified by cutting.
  Willow branches which have been peeled and bleached
  Red cockscomb
Container: Narrow chocolate-brown pottery vase

Flowing Form Using Dried Materials

A simple, single outcurve is made with dried materials.
The very long lines of the Main Stems emphasize the beauty of space.

Peacock Feathers, Bleached Fern, and Red Poppies in a Three-legged Black Iron Compote.

A twin container has been added to give a double application to the Flowing Form.

Peacock Feathers, Bleached Fern, and a Mass of Yellow Poppies in a Pair of Three-legged Black Iron Compotes.

Peach Branch, Bridal Spirea, and Calla Lilies in a Brown, Snail-shaped Vase.

The Flowing Form is best suited to a narrow, flat container, but sometimes a taller vase is desirable. When this kind of container is used, a wide sense of space must be created by using long branches that flow over the side and well beyond the edge of the container.

Instead of putting such arrangements in the middle of the area of placement, move them left or right to give the long branches plenty of room to flow outward and develop a feeling of flowing space.

Daffodil Blossoms and Leaves in an Original Rough Surfaced Black Ceramic Vase.

Bleached and Rolled Willow, Purple Heather, and Spray of Pink Orchids in a Tall White Compote.

Another Application of the Flowing Form
—Double Containers

Shortleaf Pine and Ananas in a Two-mouth Bamboo Basket with Legs.

Bleached Wild Grass and Purple and Yellow Pansies in Twin Tumblers with Glass Marbles.

The use of clear marbles in glass containers gives a dimension of depth, added beauty from reflected light, and a cool underwater feeling. Furthermore the marbles help hold the flowers firmly in place.

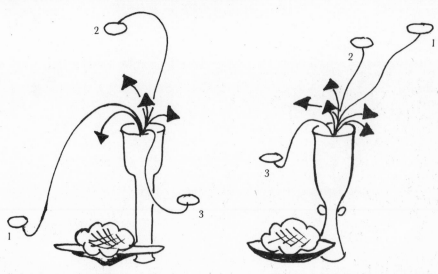

Hanging Combination Form   Slanting Combination Form

Combination Form—Two Containers
APPLIED STYLE 3

A.   Hanging Combination Form with Low Container

Tall Vase:

FIRST MAIN STEM: Place the stem at either point two or point eight in the container. Insert it in the vase so that it hangs forward; the degree of incline depends on the material used.

SECOND MAIN STEM: Place in the center of the container with the tip of the branch slanting about thirty degrees forward.

THIRD MAIN STEM: Place this stem on the side opposite the First Main Stem and slanting slightly forward.

Flat Container:
Set under the First Main Stem, this vase must contain a mass-type arrangement: it becomes an accessory to the tall vase.

B.   Slanting Combination Form with Low Container

Tall Vase:

FIRST MAIN STEM: Place this stem slanting about fifty degrees forward either at point two or eight.

SECOND MAIN STEM: Place in the center of the container, slanting about thirty degrees forward.

THIRD MAIN STEM: Place this stem opposite the First Main Stem and slanting slightly about sixty degrees forward.

Flat or Low Container:
Create a mass arrangement in this container and set it under the Third Main Stem.

Basic Flowers:
If tall containers are used with the Hanging Combination Form or the Slanting Combination Form, each Basic Flower must be a different length.

Materials:

A. Hanging Combination Form

Any material that has a natural drooping or hanging form.

B. Slanting Combination Form

Materials that have straight lines or natural curves.

Container:

Tall vase paired with a low flat container. Sometimes a very large shallow container may be used and the tall vase set in it.

Though two containers are used in this form and though the arrangements are made separately, the results must give a sense of unity and complete harmony. It is possible to use a container with two mouths, one higher than the other, or the two containers may hang at staggered levels on a wall. This combination arrangement adapts well to step or nest tables.

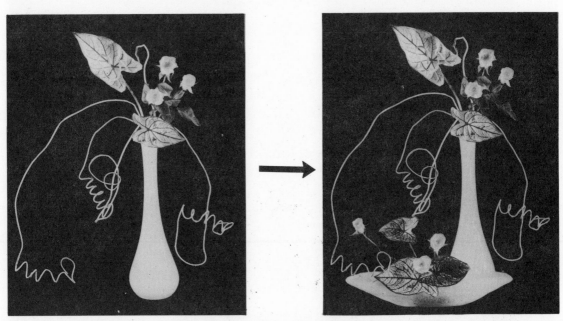

Wisteria Vine, Caladium Leaf and Roses in a Low Glass Container and a Tall Vase.

Ginger Leaves and Orange Tiger Lilies in a Tall Chinese Celadon Container with Matching Low, Boat-shaped Container.

Variations on Hanging Combination Form A

Materials: Bittersweet berries
Croton leaves
White chrysanthemums
Yellow chrysanthemums
Red baby chrysanthemums

Container: Tall, lined, glazed pottery vase
Matching flat boat-shaped container

See page 30 for Step-by-step Explanation.

Variations on Slanting Combination Form B

Materials: Ginger leaf
                  Orange tiger lilies
                  Weeping willow branches
Container: Tall Chinese celadon container with matching low, boat-shaped container.

In the photograph at the bottom of page 27 a Slanting Form B is illustrated. To create more beauty and interest, a branch of weeping willow has been used. This addition combines the Hanging Combination Form and the Slanting Combination Form in one arrangement.

STEP-BY-STEP EXPLANATION

A

STEP 1.   The First Main Stem has been placed in the tall vase on the left front at about point two. Because this material droops beautifully, it has been set to enhance this characteristic. The droop, or degree of hanging, must be adjusted to the nature of the material. After the First Main Stem is correctly placed, the flat container is moved directly under it.

B

STEP 2.   The Second Main Stem, placed in the center of the container, droops to the front.

STEP 3.   The Third Main Stem, added opposite the First Main Stem, droops low over the container.

C

STEP 4.   The Assistant Stems, three croton leaves, are added.

STEP 5   The Basic Flowers, three white chrysanthemums, one long, one of medium length, and one short, are added.

D

STEP 6.   The large yellow and the small red baby chrysanthemums add color accent to the flat container. See illustration on page 28.

Variations on the Combination Form in Two-mouth Containers

Plum Branch, Miriyo *Green Fern, and Anthurium in a Double-mouth, Brown Unglazed Vase.*

Further Variations on the Combination Form in Two-mouth Containers

Materials: Bittersweet berries
            Yellow roses
            Red roses
Container: Tall black double-mouth container

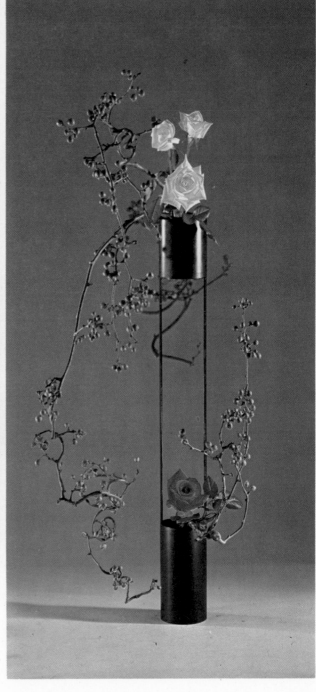

Materials: Weeping willow
            Red camellias
Container: Tall black double-mouth container

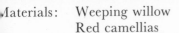

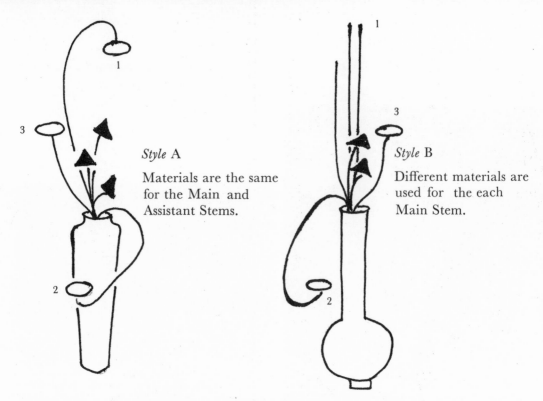

Style A

Materials are the same
for the Main and
Assistant Stems.

Style B

Different materials are
used for the each
Main Stem.

Heaven-earth Form
APPLIED STYLE 4

Style A

First Main Stem:	Place in the center of the vase. The tip of the branch slants about thirty degrees forward.
Second Main Stem:	Put in the front of the vase, it hangs down about 130 degrees. This stem combines with the First Main Stem to form a long, narrow S shape.
Third Main Stem:	Placed on the same side as the First Main Stem, this must slant about fifty degrees between the front and the side. It must follow the line and curve of the First Main Stem.
Materials:	Branches or plants with natural hanging or drooping forms.
Container:	Tall vase, wall hanger, or footed compote.

The S must create a long, narrow outline, and the Basic Flowers must rest just at the top of the container.

The outline of the First and Second Main Stems suggests Heaven and Earth tenderly caring for the flowers, and the graceful ascending and descending curves of the First and Second Main Stems form the vertical S reminiscent of the feminine beauty depicted in the Japanese dance.

This arrangement is most beautiful when set in a tall, narrow area, but it may also be set in the center of a space with accessories on either side.

Style B

Straight material is used for the First Main Stem and curved material for the Second and Third Main Stems. This gives a strong sense of contrast. Though the feeling created is stronger than that in Style A, the mood is nonetheless reminiscent of the dance.

Style A

*Dried Berries and Yellow Roses in a Smoky
Blue Glass Vase.*

Style B

*Bamboo, Bleached Broom Grass, and Red
Roses in a Three-legged Grey Ceramic
Vase.*

35

Variations on Heaven-earth Form A

See page 38 for Step-by-step Explanation.

White Quince and Yellow Chrysanthemums in a Tall White-lined Ceramic Vase.

Peeled Wisteria Vine, Grapes, Green Fern, Cockscomb, Easter Lilies, and Yellow Chrysanthemums in a Tall White Ceramic Compote.

The forms and colors of various fruits contribute to novel lines and in ikebana arrangements.

Broom Grass, Bittersweet Berries, and Gerbera Daisies in a French Wine Decanter.

STEP-BY-STEP EXPLANATION

A

STEP 1.   Although arrangements usually begin with the First Main Stem, in the Heaven-Earth Form it is easier to begin with the Second Main Stem. The white quince, curved sharply downward, has been bent and placed in the right of the container. The tip has been bent upward. If a naturally drooping branch is used, the tip may have a downward slant as well.

B

STEP 2.   A very long branch of quince is placed in the center of the container. This stem must be long enough to give a feeling of reaching upward towards heaven. Combined with the Second Main Stem, it creates the tall, narrow S.

STEP 3.   A slender branch of quince, added to the same side as the First Main Stem, gives exact upward motion and follows the outline of the First Main Stem.

C

STEP 4.   After the long, very narrow triangle has been outlined, the Basic Flowers are added in the exact center. These should be placed with great care to nestle close to the rim of the container and not to protrude or interrupt the long narrow S.

Red Quince and White Calla Lilies in an Indian Brass Water Pitcher.

Variations on the Heaven-earth Form

Style A

The lines of the container and those of the arrangement must always harmonize. The graceful spout of this pitcher curves to the left; the handle follows a leftward motion. It is natural that the branches continue this line. In fact it would violate all conceptions of ikebana line to position the stems otherwise. The attached top of the container takes the place of the Third Main Stem.

Bleached Wild Thorn Branch, Variegated Ivy, and Orchids in a Tall, Slender, Highly Glazed Vase.

More Variations on the Heaven-earth Form

Style   A

Materials bent into elaborate curves develop strong action or movement.
The First and Second Main Stems are the same material; ivy occupies the
position of the Third Main Stem.

Painted Black Broom Grass, Holly Nandina, Mitsumata, and Anthurium in a Black Porcelain Compote.

Variations on the Heaven-earth Form

Style **B**
Strong contrast results from soft curved First and Third Main Stems and the straight, strong downward line of the Second Main Stem.

The bleached limb of *mitumata* (a Japanese shrub) is turned upside down to change the natural feeling of the arrangement and thus to create an abstract design.

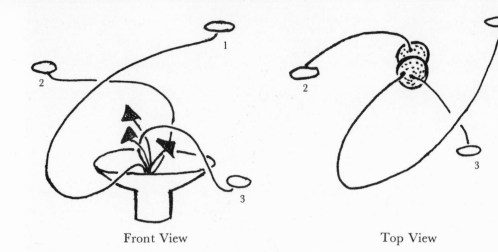

Front View   Top View

Crossing Form
APPLIED STYLE 5

FIRST MAIN STEM: The naturally curved material is placed on the left
                    of the *kenzan* to give a strong, upward, round open
                    curve.

SECOND MAIN STEM: This stem is placed exactly opposite the First Main
                    Stem so that the middle tops of the branches cross
                    each other.

THIRD MAIN STEM: This is placed between the front and side of the
                    kenzan opposite the First Main Stem and is curved
                    so that the top of this branch crosses the lower part
                    of the Second Main Stem.

Materials: Curved wisteria branches, willow, bittersweet,
                    broom grass.

    Any limber materials or branches that can be bent and curved.

Container: Adaptable to any type—low container, compote,
                    tall vase

Many variations and names are given to this form: cross-style or curve
crossing style. No matter what the name, however, the style dramatically
illustrates the importance of line. Until this·point, the beauty of line in a
single curve has been shown, but when two curves flowing in different
directions cross, a new concept of linear beauty is created.

The Crossing Forms illustrate the vitality and aesthetic importance of
contrast, an element as important to ikebana as to many other art forms.
Just as two dancers moving in contrast stimulate greater interest than a
soloist and just as the dynamic harmony of an entire orchestra is more
thrilling than the piping of a single instrument, so the crossing lines of the
branches in this form compound its aesthetic appeal. This has not always
been recognized, however, for until this century, tradition-bound rules
forbade the crossing of branches. But today, ikebana, like many other arts,
makes wider allowance for individual creativity and experimentation, and
the Ichiyo School itself, though of course rooted securely in the great
foundation of traditional ikebana, also plays an important role in the
movement to develop personalized creativity on the part of artists.

The Crossing Form is the twentieth century's contribution to an art form
many centuries old.

Baby's Breath and Hydrangea Blossoms in an Original Light-brown Two-legged Ceramic Vase.

Example of the Crossing Form

To the simple outline of the Crossing Form, Assistant Stems are added to give more depth.

In figure in the design above, the large spaces created by the outline of the three curved Main Stems are an essential part of this Crossing Form. Very long stems are needed to make sweeping curves. In measuring the branches, allow plenty of length to the Main Stems.

Pussy Willow, White Chrysanthemums, and Orange Calendulas in a Bronze Compote Designed by the author.

Illustrations of the Crossing Form

See page 47 for Step-by-step Explanation.

Scotch Broom and Red Tulips in a Leaf-shaped Container.

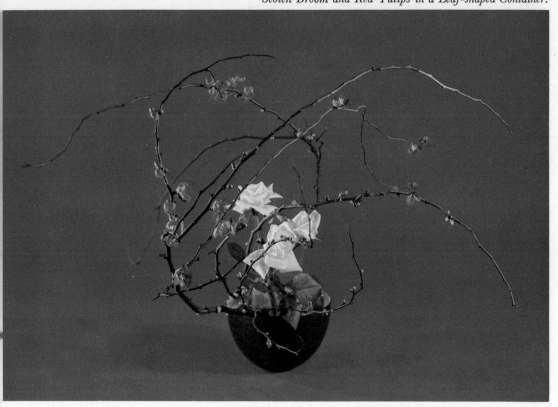

Red Quince and Light-yellow Roses in a Black Japanese Bowl.

See pages 50 and 51 for Step-by-step Explanation.

Peeled and Curved Bleached Willow, Asparagus Fern, and Purple and Yellow Pansies in a Light-pink Glass Fruit Bowl with Clear Marbles.

Variations on the Crossing Form

Many stems forming wide curves have been used to evoke the beauty of movement. Pansies, which are attractive in mass, are easier to use if tied in bunches.

Marbles cover the *kenzan*, and the addition of glass to glass intensifies the appeal of the arrangement.

Dried or bleached materials may be used in this form.

To avoid breakage when shaping the curves, soak the material for a few minutes in water to soften the stems. However, since this creates a problem of support, wire strong reinforcing stems to the bottom one or two inches of the Main Stems. This will keep them in the correct position on the *kenzan*.

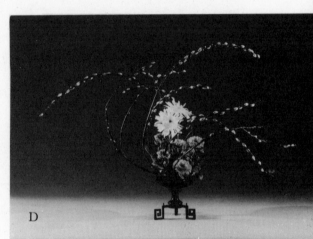

STEP-BY-STEP EXPLANATION

A
STEP 1.   Three pussy willow branches are bent and curved. The First, Second and Third Main Stems are placed in different directions so as to cross each other.

B
STEP 2.   Assistant Stems are added to each Main Stem. The Assistant Stem always moves in the same direction as its Main Stem.

C
STEP 3.   The Basic Flowers, two long-stemmed white chrysanthemums, complete the arrangement.

D
STEP 4.   Even though Step 3 could complete this arrangement further color contrast is produced by placing a mass of orange calendulas beneath the white chrysanthemums. See pages 44 and 45 for illustrations.

Bleached Willow and White Clematis in a Black-painted Bamboo Basket.

Variations on the Crossing Form
Tall Narrow Style

This variation on the Crossing Form is tall and very narrow. The Basic Flowers are placed straight in the container to emphasize this appearance. The arrangement has graceful, elegant lines, and overtones of Western flower design. The Ichiyo School seeks to assimilate color harmony, material, and feelings of all countries and to adapt them to the basic concepts, rules, and inspiration of ikebana.

Plastic Balls and Artichokes in a Malaysia's Pitcher.

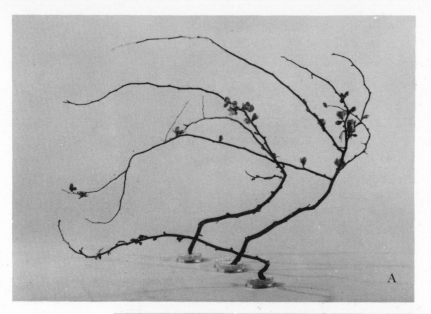
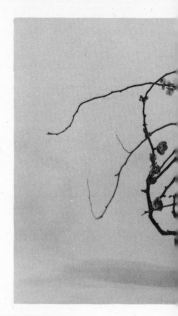

A

B

C

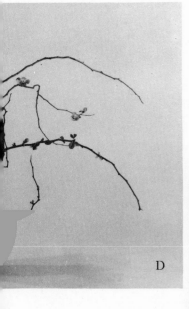

D

E

STEP-BY-STEP EXPLANATION

A

STEP 1.   Before beginning this arrangement, consider ways of crossing the branches, which are aligned in the illustration to facilitate studying their possibilities. Since the sides of the deep container will interrupt the lines of the branches in their most powerfully moving directions, it is best to bend their lower sections at points as far from their ends as the depth of the container. Bent this way and inserted in the vase, they will stand firmly on the *kenzan*.

B

STEP 2.   The longest stem is placed in the container as shown.

C

STEP 3.   The Second Main Stem must form a wide, open, upward curve. Viewed from the front, the stems will cross each other.

D

STEP 4.   The Third Main Stem is in place. Each of the Main Stems has an auxiliary branch on the main bough which acts as an Assistant Stem. Curve them by hand to follow the lines of the Main Stems. Even without Basic Flowers, this is a beautiful arrangement.

E

STEP 5.   The roses, the Basic Flowers, complete the design. See illustrations on page 45.

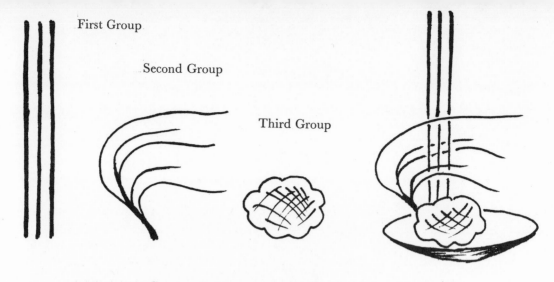

First Group

Second Group

Third Group

Group-contrast Form

APPLIED STYLE 6

FIRST GROUP: This group of stems is placed upright on the *kenzan*.
SECOND GROUP: This group, which curves in a semi-circle, must be set
               on the *kenzan* so that it crosses the first group.
THIRD GROUP: This low mass is placed to give both line and color
               contrast.
Materials: Straight, semicircular, short stemmed.
Container: Low container, compote, or tall vase.

This form is the transitional step to advanced ikebana. Three different
groups of materials are placed, not stem by stem, but in bunches according
to the formation or line characteristic of the material itself. The steps of
construction are simple, but the choice of materials creates the beauty.

Cattails, Wisteria Vines, and Yellow Chrysanthemums in a Low, Heart-shaped
   Container with Three Legs.

Instead of lightness and delicacy, this form attempts to produce a sense of strength and weight by means of contrasting formation and application of materials. The power of the arrangement is derived from the lines of the materials, but a sense of balance and harmony must pervade the effect. To continue the analogy between flowers and performing arts, this form suggests groups of dancers, choruses, or full orchestras.

Cattails, Orange-dyed Broom Grass, White Pampas Grass, and Red Cockscomb in an Oval, Two-colored Pottery Vase.

Variations on Group-contrast Form

The tall straight lines of the cattails combine with the tall soft, though also straight, pampas grass. In contrast of form and color, the dried broom grass is shaped into a semicircle and placed on the *kenzan* in front of the cattails and pampas grass. The cockscombs are of two lengths and are placed stairstep fashion behind the broom grass.

A

C

Mitsumata, *Black Pussy Willow, and Orange Calendulas in a Dark Orange, Wave-shaped Pottery Vase.*

B

STEP-BY-STEP EXPLANATION

A
STEP 1.   The *mitsumata* in the first group is inserted upright. Interest is added by inverting one branch.
B
STEP 2.   The addition of the curved black willow creates contrast of line and color.
C
STEP 3.   Short-stemmed orange calendulas close together at the base of the arrangement contribute mass.

Red Maple Branches, Holly Nandima, and Light Yellow Chrysanthemums in a Large Shallow Round White Bowl.

To increase contrast with the tall maple and to strengthen and stabilize the lines, the tops of the branches are cut straight across.

Japanese Iris, Large-leaf Maple, and Baby's Breath in a Pale-green off-center Compote.

Variation on the Group-contrast Form

The same technique used in the Group-contrast Form is applied in this arrangement, but taller materials are chosen to give a long, upreaching feeling. The imaginative aim is to create the cool sensation of a summer pondside. The seasons play a predominate role in all Japanese flower creations.

Calla Lilies and Red Quince in a Green Compote.

In sharp contrast to the natural traditional feeling of the arrangement on the opposite page, this modern one uses calla lilies at the top and the base and a strongly curved branch of quince, which by filling the space between the calla lilies, suggests strong emotion.

A close study of these two illustrations reveals the difference made by choice and use of materials. The soft color and line crossing on the left as well as the strong curve and color contrast in the arrangement above show how imagination and creativeness elevate modern ikebana to the highest artistic plane.

In strictly traditional ikebana, plants must never be arranged in opposition to their natural growth; at present, however, the rules of nature may be altered to express the creative ideas of the arranger.

Preparing Leaves and Flowers for Arrangement

Ikebana materials last longer and keep their natural colors and freshness over a greater period of time if submitted to one of the following simple processes: the Physical Method or the Chemical Method.

Physical Method:

1. CARE IN GATHERING FLOWERS

Gather flowers from the garden in the early morning or late evening when the moisture in the plant cells is at the highest and the evaporation point lowest. Wild flowers and plants or flowers that wilt and fade quickly must be placed in water as soon as they are cut. Put the freshly cut flowers in a weak sugar-water solution and set them in a cool, dark, draftless place for an hour or longer to revive.

2. CUTTING UNDER WATER

Submerge stems and cut off an inch or two from their ends while holding them under water. This keeps the air from blocking the exposed end so that water can be freely absorbed; it is the easiest and most effective method for increasing the life span of most leaves and flowers.

Cutting Under Water

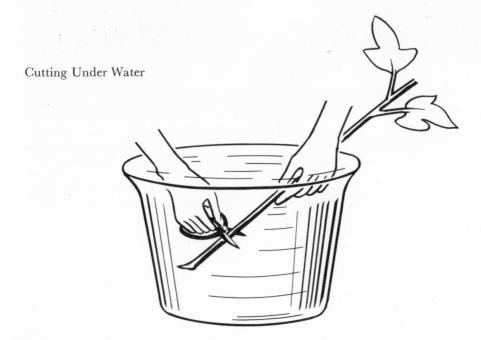

3. BREAKING, CRUSHING, AND SHAVING

These methods are applicable to woody materials. Break the stem of a branch near the root. If it is very thick, shave off the bark around the bottom portion to expose more water-absorbing surface. If the stem is thin with a small water absorbing area, crush its end.

4. BURNING

This method is used for fuzzy and milky-stemmed flowers, such as peonies, geraniums, plum blossoms, spireas, and chrysanthemums. Hold the cut end of the stem over a gas burner or candle flame until it is very hot. Immediately plunge the scared stem into deep cold water. This will preserve the end of the stem from quick decay.

Burning

5. BOILING

This method preserves flowering plants, stock, lily of the valley, poinsettia, hydrangea, rose, balloon flower, dahlia, and thistle. Soak the roots of the flowers in boiling salt water for a minute or two until the green of the stem begins to lighten. Place them immediately into deep cool water.

In both the burning and boiling methods, utmost care must be taken to protect the leaves and flowers from being exposed to direct heat. The best protection is to wrap them in wet newspaper with only the cut ends of the stems exposed to the heat or boiling water.

Boiling

Chemical Method :

Break or crush the end of the stem and immerse it in the appropriate chemical for a few minutes. Several stems may be held in the chemical at one time. Dry the cut end of the stem before it is put into liquid chemicals.

1. ACIDS: *vinegar, acetic acid, acetate,* or *diluted hydrochloric acid.*
   Materials: reed, bamboo, pampas grass, sage, banana tree, etc.

2. ALKALIES: *salt*
   Materials: camellia, Chinese bell flower
   Ashes
   Materials: bulrush, calla lily, water lily, etc.

3. STIMULANTS: *sugar, red pepper, essence of peppermint.*
   Materials: flowering plants.

Dip the stems of tulips in sugar before inserting them on the *kenzan*, and sprinkle about one teaspoon on the *kenzan*.

4. ALCOHOL, LIQUORS.
Materials: lilac, wisteria, maple, gerbera daisy, poppy, aster, narcissus.

Pumping Method

A specially designed pump is often used to inject water or chemicals into the stems of materials that do not absorb easily: water plants, such as lotus and water lily.

Pumping Method

Tips For Keeping Arrangements Fresh

1.   Always use a clean container and *kenzan*. They must be washed in warm, soapy water, rinsed thoroughly, dried, and stored carefully after each use.

2.   After an arrangement is completed, the water in the container must be changed daily. This is especially important during the summer months. To prevent disturbing the arrangement, a rubber tube may be used to withdraw the old water and to refill with fresh. Ice cubes may be added in hot weather.

3.   As often as possible, recut the ends of the stems under water and replace them in the container as before. This renews the cut surface for better absorption.

4.   Arrangements in deep containers tend to last longer. Materials placed in a deep tub or bucket for a time will be revived by the pressure of the water.

5.   Leaves breathe from the undersides. Holding the flowers upside down, wash off the dust to help plants breathe better and stay fresh and green longer.

6.   Spray the flowers, or completed arrangement, with a fine mist. This replenishes the moisture in the leaf and is very important in the summer when moisture evaporates quickly. Moreover, a fine mist on the flowers looks like dew or rain droplets and creates a sense of freshness and coolness.

Preserving Leaves

1.   Remove all excess leaves from the branches or stems of flowers. This allows the water to be used for only those necessary to the composition.

2.   Large leaves, like those of calla lilies, droop and wilt quickly. While retaining the original shape of the leaf, trim the edges to make them smaller. Wash the leaves daily to restore their moisture.